To Clay

Good fishing! Don't let life's big ones get away.

Four Weeks With God and Your Neighbor

A Devotional Workbook for Counselees and Others

by
Jay E. Adams

Presbyterian and Reformed Publishing Co.

PRINTED IN THE UNITED STATES OF AMERICA

ISBN: 0-87552-020-0

About This Book

This devotional book is unique. By leafing through it you will see from its format that it is unlike any devotional book you have ever seen before. Here are its special features:

1. There are only five devotional studies per week (for Monday through Friday).
2. Saturday is set aside as a time for review, evaluation, and consolidation of gains.
3. Sunday's page is designed for directed note-taking at church, leading to application of the preacher's sermons.
4. The morning weekday studies require study and lead toward personal application during the day.
5. The evening checkup provides opportunity to see progress and growth in the use of Scripture in daily life.

The devotional workbook originally was designed for use with counselees to accompany and supplement counseling. It is important for counselees who are involved in scriptural counseling to back up the counseling itself with daily study, prayer, and application that will undergird all else. Building good devotional patterns is important. Since an adequate devotional book could not be found for the purpose, this one was developed. It covers a four-week period— roughly the time necessary for a counselee (or anyone else) to establish new patterns. The assignments in the workbook attempt to bring about this result.

While the devotional workbook was designed as a handout for counselees, it surely may be used by any Christian who is seeking a more meaningful and more productive devotional experience. It may be used alone, by families, by groups, etc. Flexibility has been built in. But when used by more than one, the assignments and the evaluations ought to be done and recorded individually, or a large part of the value will be lost.

When you have completed the four weeks, take the time each week thereafter for at least four more weeks to read (and reread) once each week (at one sitting) all that you recorded in your workbook. In this way you will be reminded of commitments, changes, gains, struggles, problems, principles, promises, etc., that you ought not to forget. Of course, this rereading ought not to be substituted for further daily devotional work. A good time to reread might be each Sunday afternoon.

I have chosen quite reluctantly to use the words *devotion* and *devotional*. Frequently, I have discovered, the words connote (if they haven't come to denote) a superficial, mystical reading of the Bible (without understanding) mixed with prayer. Nothing could be further from my mind. While Bible reading and prayer form a part of this four-week program, they are done from the perspective of knowledge and understanding. The Bible is not a mystical book; it does not intend to mystify but to give knowledge and wisdom for life. Christians are not mystics. The purpose of the Bible, Christ said, was to enable people to love God and their neighbors. That is practical, not mystical.

Each day's morning work should take about half an hour. The evening work may be done in as little as fifteen minutes (it may take longer if there are problems from the day that must be dealt with).

ALWAYS BEGIN USING THIS WORKBOOK ON A MONDAY. BEGIN WITH WEEK ONE. DO NOT SKIP ANY LESSONS. IF YOU MISS A DAY, SPEND EXTRA TIME THE NEXT DAY CATCHING UP. ONE DAY BUILDS ON ANOTHER.

Week One   Monday

Morning

1. Pray (briefly) for God to instruct you as you study.
2. Read Ephesians 4:17-24 in a modern translation (but not in a paraphrase). As you read, jot down key personal applications of truths in the passage that are immediately apparent. A *Bible truth* is a warning, promise, command or example. An *application* is a way to put the warning or promise to use, to obey the command or to follow the example.

   To get started on the four-week program here is a little help in filling out the applications (A-H). Sins are the violation of the Ten Commandments, either directly or as they are explicated in other commands and warnings. One may sin by omission and commission; the Commandments can be broken in thought as well as in deed. Look for opportunities to apply these biblical truths at work, school, home, in contact with a neighbor, etc. Especially look for simple recurring situations requiring small changes. Do not bite off more than you can chew.

Applications to My Life:

A _____

B _____

C _____

D _____

E _____

3. Read the following and (again) jot down all additional applications to your life:

You Must Change

God everywhere in the Scriptures commands *change:* "As children who are under obedience, don't shape your live by the desires that you used to follow in your ignorance. Instead, as the One Who called you is holy, you yourselves must become holy in all your behavior" (I Peter 1:14, 15); "You must no longer walk like the Gentiles do" (Ephesians 4:17); "Grow by the help and the knowledge of our Lord and Savior Jesus Christ" (II Peter 3:18).[1] You could go on and on, but these three samples establish what you already know to be true.

At first, such demands for change may seem discouraging: "I have so much changing to do," you may think. Doubtless that is true, but what you may not have realized is that every biblical exhortation, every insistence upon change, implies hope. God never demands of His children that which He is not willing and able to provide for them. Both facts are certain: (1) you have great changes to make; (2) you have a greater God Who has great resources for change. You are not only *saved* by grace, but your sanctification (i.e., your continued change from sin toward righteousness) also is the result of God's grace. Remember, Paul told the Galatians that we did not begin the Christian life by grace, only to complete it by our own efforts (Galatians 3:3). No, *all*—all change—takes place by grace. All progress in your Christian life will be brought about by God through His Spirit as you are willing to obey His Word in faith. That means, therefore, that God Himself has provided both the *instructions* and the *power* to live according to them. The *instructions*—the goals, values, principles and practices—are found in the Scriptures; the *power* for Christians to live by them is provided by His Spirit. That is the good news from God's Word for you today.

Applications for My Life:

F _____

G _____

---

1. All quotations are from *The N.T. in Everyday English* unless otherwise noted.

H _____

4. From the applications listed above (A-H), select one—perhaps the one that seems easiest to accomplish (don't attempt more than you can do and become discouraged at the outset)—and throughout this day look for opportunities to apply this scriptural truth to your relationship with God and others.
5. List one possible situation in which you anticipate that this truth might be activated and think concretely about *how* you would apply it. State your plan for applying the truth (in an if . . . then form) below:

Application Plan:

If _____

_____ [occurs],

then I plan to _____

_____

6. Ask God to bless your plan (or to show you where it is wrong if it is).

Evening Checkup

1. Reread your notes from this morning; then answer the following questions:

   a) Did the situation I anticipated occur? _____

   b) If so, did I follow my plan? _____

   c) What was the outcome? _____

   _____

d) In what other ways did I apply the Bible truth I selected?

_____

2. In the space below, make comments on how well (or poorly) you

did: _____

_____

_____

3. If you failed, try to determine (1) what was behind the failure?

_____

_____ and (2) what God wants

you to do to rectify the situation and to overcome it in the future.

_____

_____

(If you are in counseling, you may wish to discuss this with your
counselor at the next session.)

4. Pray about the whole matter, seeking forgiveness where necessary,
thanking God for successes (even if all that you did was to make
genuine efforts; this itself, don't forget, is the first step in the
right direction). Ask for strength and help for tomorrow.

Week One   Tuesday

Morning

1. Remember yesterday's work and last night's evaluation of it; in the light of this, ask God's blessing and help upon today's study and application.
2. Today, you want to build on yesterday's work. Whether you failed or succeeded in obeying God's Word, continue to be conscious of the biblical principle you learned and any concrete applications that you planned, and continue to follow this plan[1] along with the new one that grows out of today's study.
3. Read the following Scripture passage: II Timothy 3 (the whole chapter). Jot down truths to be applied to your life:

A _____

B _____

C _____

D _____

E _____

4. Read the following and jot down any other applications that come to mind:

Four Things the Bible Does for You

To be specific, just what *does* the Bible provide? Let us look closely at II Timothy 3:15-17 to see.

---

1. Change or revise it if necessary, of course.

In this fundamental passage concerning the Scriptures, it is important first to note that their twofold "use" or "purpose" is described *in terms of change:*

(1) Salvation: The Scriptures alone are able to make one "wise unto salvation (life's greatest change—from death to spiritual life) through faith in Christ";

(2) for those who *are* saved, the Scriptures provide four things:

    (a) **Teaching**—they become the standard for faith and life; they show us all that God requires of us.

    (b) **Conviction**—they show us how we have failed to measure up to those requirements in our lives. This second word is a legal term meaning more than to "rebuke" or "accuse," but speaks of pursuing a court case *successfully.* It means "to be convicted of the crime of which one has been accused." The Bible *convicts* us of sin. The Scriptures flatten us in repentance.

    (c) **Correction**—the word means (literally) "to stand up straight again." While it is true that the Bible knocks us down, cuts and bruises, rips up and tears down, it is equally true that this is done only to prepare us for its work of picking us up and heading us in God's proper direction. The Scriptures also bind up and heal. They plant and build. By God's Spirit, who works in and through them, they not only help us put off sin, but also enable us to put on righteousness.

    (d) **Training in righteousness**—it isn't enough to quit the past ways, break old habits and stop sinning. When that's all that happens, you soon find yourself reverting to past ways. You must also learn to walk in God's new scriptural paths *as a way of life.*

    And what does all of this amount to? Change. We have just been describing the process of *change.* Change in depth. Change as profound as one could imagine. Eternal change. And it is all found in God's Book, the textbook on change, the Bible.

Applications to My Life:

F _____

G _____

H _____

5. Again, select one truth that you will consciously carry with you throughout the day (along with yesterday's), looking for contexts in which God expects you to apply it.
6. Once more, lay out a plan for concretely applying this truth in at least one anticipated situation:

Application Plan:

If _____

_____ [occurs],

then I plan to _____

_____

7. General prayer time. But also pray especially for today's growth in the application of the two biblical principles you are learning to apply.

Evening Checkup

1. How did you do? Reread your notes for yesterday and today and make an evaluation of your progress, listing successes, partial successes, failures, along with what you did (or didn't do) that brought the success/failure:

_____

_____

_____

_____

7

2. What does God want you to do tomorrow (1) to overcome your

   failures? _____

   _____

   _____

   _____ (2) to consolidate your gains?

   _____

   _____

   _____

3. Talk to God, as you did yesterday, about today's work.
4. If you persist in failing (and don't know why), jot down all perti-
   nent facts and bring these to the next counseling session to discuss with your counselor (for others not in counseling: if after
   a week's failure on the same item you see no gains, make an
   appointment with your pastor to discuss the matter).

Week One   Wednesday

Morning

1. Good morning! God has given you a fresh new day in which to grow, and ask for His strength. Thank Him and take full advantage of it.
2. Here's today's passage: I Samuel 16:6-13. Again, jot down truths and their applications to your life:

A _____

B _____

C _____

D _____

E _____

3. Read this too:

What Is Your Motive?

The area of motive is planted thickly with thorny questions. I shall mention but one. While, on the one hand, Christians must inquire about and discuss motives, on the other hand they are incapable of judging motives. God alone can judge the heart. Man looks only on the outward appearance. Suppose you have done your best to explain the proper biblical motivation behind a proposed plan of action to your counselor (or some other Christian). He has stressed the need for sincerity and warned against proceeding from lesser motivation, but then he must prayerfully leave the outcome to God.

Let us take an example. Pat, a professing Christian, goes to a Christian pastor, highly motivated to win back her husband, who has just left home. She begs, "I'll do anything to get Larry back! Just tell me what to do." The alert counselor will be wary of her *motives*, as well as her *objectives*. And if her words may be taken literally, when she says "I'll do anything . . . ," then he knows also that her strong desire would lead her to adopt non-biblical *methods* for achieving her end. He will soon bring the discussion around to goals and motives. He will say something like this: "Pat, as a Christian your goal must be to please God, regardless of the consequences. You must be willing to lose Larry if in the providence of God that should be the outcome. You cannot do what the Bible says simply as a technique or gimmick to get him back. It's true that if anything will bring Larry home again, it will be Christian behavior on your part, but you must not change primarily for that reason. What God requires of you at this time must be done—*whether Larry returns or not*. You must do it out of genuine repentance and love for God. If Larry returns, then your secondary hope will be realized; but even if he doesn't, when your primary hope has been to please God, you will not be disappointed in it; and only then will you be in a proper condition to handle your other disappointments. At bottom the only scriptural motive for action is to please God. You must change for that reason.

Truths and Applications:

F _____

G _____

H _____

4. If you have been succeeding well with your work so far, select *two* truths and lay out concrete plans for consciously putting them into effect today. If things have not been going so well, continue to add only *one* new truth, and lay out *one* new plan each day:

A. If _____

_____ [occurs],

then I plan to _____

_____

B. If _____

_____ [occurs],

then I plan to _____

_____

5. General prayer time (be sure you pray for others too; it is easy to become self-centered when working on problems in your own life. Remember, your goal in all this work is to learn how to love God and your neighbor in new ways). Ask for help to overcome previous problems as well as to grow in loving obedience to His Word. Pray about your motives in all of this.

Evening Checkup

1. Check up on all that you have learned this week so far. How are you doing? Has there been growth? If so, list what and how it happened (don't miss a thing):

_____

_____

_____

2. Have there been failures? What have you done about them?

_____

What else (if anything) does God want you to do? _____

_____

_____

3. Talk it over with God (don't worry about "thee's" and "thou's"
   in prayer. Just talk to God in your normal everyday language,
   understanding Who it is to Whom you are speaking and main-
   taining all due respect).

Morning

1. This is your fourth day! Are you excited? Growing restless? Confused? Discouraged? Convicted? It wouldn't be unusual for you to have experienced a number (or all) of these things by now. There will be ups and downs. But, remember, the crucial thing to do is to continue using this workbook each day NO MATTER HOW YOU FEEL. Don't follow feelings; follow God's responsibilities. So, then, get to work—however you feel.
2. Pray.
3. Read today's Scripture portion (and take your usual notes): Galatians 5:13-26.

Truths and Applications:

A _____

B _____

C _____

D _____

E _____

4. Now, read this:

Led by the Spirit

Being Spirit "led" (Romans 8:14) is closely connected with "putting to death the deeds of the body by the Spirit" (vs. 13). A son of God is one who, by the shepherdly work of the Spirit, is led in the paths of righteousness. He is being led to walk in new ways by putting off old sinful habit practices (the old person) and in their place is producing the fruit of the Spirit (the new person). Paul says that you can tell a believer by observing the process of sanctification (putting off sin and putting on righteousness) at work within him. You know the Spirit is present in those in whom His work is evident.

In Galatians 5:16, Paul commands, "Walk by the Spirit and it is certain that you won't accomplish the desires of the flesh." It is the Spirit who effectively enables the believer to keep the desires of the flesh (sinful responses that the body, through habit, finds easy to do) from issuing into the "deeds of the flesh." This He does by leading him into new biblical patterns appropriate to the new walk of a child of God. Another way to put it is to say that the believer is *led* by the Spirit to produce the "fruit of the Spirit."

The process of sanctification is always in view when Paul writes of the Spirit *leading*. There is not the slightest idea of special revelation, impressions, feelings or any other subjective method of guidance. The passages don't speak about decision-making. Rather, both passages that deal with leading (Romans 8:12-14; Galatians 5:16-18) have to do with the power of the Spirit that enables the believer to overcome the desires of the flesh and learn new scriptural patterns of life.

Truths and Applications:

F _____

G _____

H _____

5. Continue to select one (or two, if you are doing well) truths and lay out an applicatory plan:

A. If _____

_____ [occurs],

then I plan to _____

_____

14

B. If _____

_____ [occurs],

then I plan to _____

_____

By now you ought to be learning a bit about (1) how to discover truths in the Scriptures, (2) how to plan to anticipate difficulties, and (3) how to apply truths to everyday life situations. If you are especially weak in one of these three areas, begin to focus upon and devote more time to it.

6. General prayer time. Prayer consists of Adoration (telling God you love Him and why—with emphasis upon what He *is*), Confession (of your sin), Thanksgiving (even for difficulties), and Supplication (asking God for biblically legitimate things): ACTS.

Evening Checkup

1. Write out an evaluation of the day's progress, listing gains and losses, what was behind each and what God wants you to do about it:

_____

_____

_____

_____

_____

2. If important to do so, make notes on problems to take to your next counseling session (or to ask your pastor or another Christian about).
3. Read today's Scripture portion again, then close in prayer that is appropriate.

15

Week One   Friday

Morning

1. Well! You've come to the end of your first week's effort. Today, you will read one more passage and follow one more assignment. Tomorrow and the next day will be different. Ask God to help you close this work week well.
2. Read and jot down truths/applications: Romans 6:1-23.

A _____

B _____

C _____

D _____

E _____

3. Then read the following and do the same:

Your Flesh and You

"Flesh," whenever Paul uses it in a negative sense, means a *body habituated* to the ways of the world rather than to the ways of God. The idea of bodily habituation frequently appears. The *flesh* is the "former manner of life" or "previous habits," also referred to as the "old self" in Ephesians 4:22. It is the "old self with his *practices*" in Colossians 3:9. It is the sinful ways that have been programmed and patterned into life by our sinful natures through continuous "yielding" of the "members" of the body to sin (Romans 6:13, 19). Before salvation, the Christian was a willing slave who offered the members of his body as instruments to carry out the wishes of his master, sin. Now, with the same willingness, he must

16

learn instead to yield the members of his body to God (cf. also Romans 12:1).

The power of habit is great. It is not easy to please God in a body that is still in part habituated by sin. Though you may wish inwardly to cease lying, to control your tongue, to stop losing your temper, or to eliminate scores of other vices, you will find that the battle against the habituated desires of the body is hard. There are victories, but they do not all come easily. Indeed, in your own strength you will fail to win the struggle. But that is not the dismal conclusion of the matter, since both in Galatians 5 and in Romans 8, as we have seen, Paul plainly points to the way to the change that pleases God.

Truths and Applications:

F _____

G _____

H _____

4. Once more, select one or two (no more) biblical truths to put to work in your life today. Plan ahead for their use:

A. If _____

_____ [occurs],

then I plan to _____

_____

B. If _____

_____ [occurs],

then I plan to _____

_____

17

5. Incidentally, by now you may have discovered (1) that things don't always happen as you anticipate; (2) that your plans must be *adapted* to fit what does happen; (3) that even when things occur quite differently, having taken time to think about a plan and having a plan to adapt is better than having nothing at all to rely on.
6. General prayer.

Evening Checkup

1. Don't spend much time tonight checking up in detail.
2. Instead, focus mainly upon talking to God about your day.

It's been quite a week! If you've worked diligently and regularly, continually asking God to give you the strength to do as He requires in His Word, you will have gained much[1]—even if many of your specific plans failed. The diligence, the fellowship with God in His Word and in prayer, the self-evaluation and the regularity are gains in themselves. Be sure you thank Him for these.

Get a good night's sleep; you have some significant, new work to do tomorrow.

---

1. Notice, the strength often comes in *faithful obedient doing* (James 1:25b; Luke 17:14).

Week One　　　　Saturday
(Any convenient time)
EVALUATION DAY!

1. Think back over the week. Pray about everything that comes to mind.
2. By now you have worked on putting five to eight biblical truths to work in your life. If you have succeeded *at all,* there will be changes in your life. Now first of all—so that we don't get all caught up in the process and forget what it's supposed to achieve —let's see *if* you've changed (and *how*).
3. List ways in which you've changed (grown). Include small changes. At first they won't be large:

_____

_____

_____

_____

_____

_____

_____

_____

_____

_____

_____

4. What was the greatest change? _____

_____

5. What brought this change about? _____

_____

6. How did you fail to change (or how did you change for the worse)? _____

_____

7. What was behind this failure? _____

_____

8. What have you done about it? _____

_____

9. What—if anything—does God still expect you to do about it?

_____

_____

_____

_____

_____

_____

_____

10. Review the work you did during the previous five days (read every page carefully). From your daily evening checkups and from your present perspective, grade each day's work (literally write out below "good, fair or poor"):

	Grades	*Comments*
Monday		
Tuesday		
Wednesday		
Thursday		
Friday		

11. Then:
   A. Pray about the evaluations you have just done.
   B. Lay plans for today and tomorrow to do whatever yet needs to be done.
12. Close in prayer.

* * * * *

When you take this workbook to your next counseling session, show the evaluation on these three pages to your counselor.

Preview tomorrow's assignment by glancing over it at
this time so that you can plan your day accordingly.

Week Two   Sunday

1. Sunday! Time for a fresh start. There is no better way than to get dressed, pray and go to church (take this book along).

2. Church School—relax; keep this book closed; take no notes.

3. *Morning Service:*

    A. Jot down any truths or applications that appear in the Scripture reading and in the sermon:

    1 _____

    2 _____

    3 _____

    4 _____

    5 _____

    B. What was the *purpose* of the sermon (i.e., how did the preacher intend to change you)? _____

    _____

4. Afternoon (at home): What truth from the above list would be a guiding principle to apply to your life throughout the coming week? (list by number) _____.

    How? _____

    _____

5. *Evening Service:*

Do the same as you did this morning under 3A and 3B:
A. Truths and applications:

1 _____

2 _____

3 _____

4 _____

5 _____

B. Purpose of the sermon:

_____

_____

6. Spend time tonight before going to sleep, asking God's blessing on
   the week to come. Look forward, not backward: this is the first
   day of the next week of your life!

Morning

1. Good morning! Today is the beginning of another work week. Thank God for the opportunity to work, and ask Him to help you serve *Him* this week in your work (quickly read Colossians 3:23-25).
2. You cannot serve Christ unless you serve like Christ. But to do so you must become like Him—i.e., you must become a godly, godlike person. Read and memorize I Timothy 4:7b: "Discipline yourself for godliness."
3. Think about this passage and write out several ways that you need to discipline yourself for godliness.

A _____

B _____

C _____

D _____

E _____

4. Now, consider the following:

Love God by Becoming Like Him

There has been some change, some growth, some blessing, but perhaps not the kind that you so earnestly wanted. Since that is the experience of many Christians, you are not alone. Some have given up the hope of ever becoming significantly different. Yet there *are* some Christians whose lives are different. If they have found the answer, you can too. You have the same God, the same Bible and the same power available as they. Yet, there is one difference between you and them.

What is it? Why do you rarely succeed in changing even in small ways? There must be something wrong. You *want* the right thing, yet so rarely achieve it. Of course, there may be many reasons for this. At the bottom is sin. But here look at one major reason (possibly *the* major reason) why the gears don't seem to mesh as they should. You may have sought and tried to obtain *instant* godliness. There is no such thing. Today we have instant pudding, instant coffee, instant houses shipped on trucks, instant everything. And we want instant godliness as well. We want three easy steps to godliness; but godliness doesn't come that way.

The Bible tells how godliness does come: you must *discipline yourself* toward godliness" (I Timothy 4:7). Discipline is the secret behind godliness.

The word *discipline* has all but disappeared from our culture. Yet, discipline is the only path to godliness. So you must learn to discipline yourself toward godliness.

Notice there is no option to being godly; God commands it. He commands, "Be holy as I am holy," and "Be perfect as I am perfect." You will never reach perfection in this life (I John 1:8), but perfect godliness is the goal toward which you must discipline yourself and toward which you must move every day. Godliness means becoming more like God Himself each day.

God tells you to discipline yourself *"toward* godliness." The original means *"with an orientation toward* godliness." Your whole life ought to be disciplined (i.e., structured, set up, organized, and running day by day) toward the goal of godliness. Everything you do Monday through Sunday should move you closer to that goal.

F _____

G _____

5. Which areas of your life will you begin to discipline today? _____

_____

How (state specifically)? _____

_____

6. Pray about the commitments you are making; ask God to bless you in them. Ask Him to help you remember them throughout the day and the days to come.

Evening Checkup

1. Well, how did it go today? (write out your answer): _____

_____

_____

2. From the above answer:
   A. Ask forgiveness, if necessary.
   B. Give thanks as appropriate.
   C. Request help where needed.
3. Plan to put into practice from now on what you have learned today. Be concrete in your plans (state how, what, when *specifically*):

_____

_____

_____

_____

4. Close in a brief prayer of commitment.

Week Two   Tuesday

Morning:

1. Tuesday! You are already into the thick of this week. Problems and trials abound. But, never fear, God designs each one for your personal benefit. (Read James 1:2-5 and take heart!)
2. Today's text: Luke 9:23-26. Notice, a disciple must take up his cross *daily*. The cross is an instrument of death. To deny (*lit.* "say no to") one's self is to put to death all desires that conflict with Christ's commands.
3. What desires of yours must be crucified today by saying no to them?

A _____

B _____

C _____

D _____

E _____

F _____

4. Don't fool yourself (as many do) by calling sinful desires "needs!" True needs are relatively few (I Timothy 6:8).

Discipline Is Daily

When your life is focused upon godliness, the goal will constantly come into your mind. You will think at work, at home, or in school, "What I am doing must reflect God."

When Paul writes, "You are a new creature; all things have become new," this is what he has in mind: the Holy Spirit has oriented

27

you toward God, putting a new focus on all of life. But that doesn't automatically make you godly. Because of the work of Christ you have been *counted* perfect in God's sight, but in actuality you are still far from the goal. Yet, your new life in Christ is oriented toward godliness; that is why at times you ache for it.

The very word *discipline* makes it clear that godliness can't be whipped up like instant pudding. Discipline means work; it means *sustained daily effort*. The word is a term related to athletics. An athlete becomes an expert only by years of hard practice. There are no instant athletes.

No weight lifter says, "Here is a very heavy weight. I never lifted weights before, but that looks like the largest one. I'll try to press it." He is likely to break his back. He must start out with a small weight the first week, then gradually over the months and years add heavier and heavier ones. Nor does he say, "I'll lift weights for five hours on Friday and then forget about it for the next six weeks." Athletes must practice regularly, every day. They work daily, day after day, until what they are doing is "natural" (i.e., second nature) to them. Continued daily effort is an essential element of Christian *discipline*.

G _____

H _____

5. If you have run into difficulties in putting your truths into action so far, consider whether you may have given up too quickly. Godliness comes through discipline; discipline involves regularity and repetition (daily effort). Are you undisciplined and (as a result) ungodly? Respond honestly to yourself before God:

_____

_____

6. Talk to God about your response. By now you should know how. Ask His forgiveness for giving in to your discouragements by giving up on your responsibilities. Promise Him you will be more regular in living for Him. Plan this day to do so.

Evening Checkup:

1. Well, how did it go? If "just a little better," don't be discouraged. The athlete does only a little better at each practice. But over the long haul there is large improvement. You are working on disciplined progress and growth.
2. Pray for:

    A. Patience in: _____

    B. Endurance in: _____

3. In this space list questions you may wish to ask your counselor at the next meeting:

    1 _____

    _____

    2 _____

    _____

    3 _____

    _____

    4 _____

    _____

    5 _____

    _____

    6 _____

    _____

    7 _____

Week Two   Wednesday

Morning

1. It is Wednesday already. You have been thinking about discipline and how it leads to godliness. How are you doing? Read Hebrews 5:13, 14.

Truths and Applications:

A _____

B _____

C _____

D _____

2. Then look at this:

Discipline

When a Christian daily orients his life toward godliness through discipline, something happens; something truly amazing takes place. New godly ways become as natural as walking down the street. That is the way that God made us.

God gave you a marvelous capacity called *habit*. Whenever you do something long enough, it becomes a part of you. For example, did you button your shirt up or down today? You don't think about where to begin any more; you just *do* it. You don't consciously say to yourself, "Now, I'm going to button my shirt this morning; I shall begin at the top." You don't think about that at all. You just do it without thinking about it. That is the capacity that God gave you.

How do you learn? By practice, *disciplined* practice. You drove the car long enough that driving became a part of you. It became second nature to you. That is what Paul was talking about when he spoke of godliness through discipline.

The writer of Hebrews also speaks clearly about this matter (5: 13ff.). There he is upbraiding the Hebrew Christians because, although they had received much teaching from God's Word, they had not profited from it. The reason was that they had not *used* it. Consequently, when they ought to have become teachers, they still needed to be taught. He says that "everyone who feeds on milk is *inexperienced* with the righteous Word; he is still a baby" (verse 13). He continues: "Solid food [meat and potatoes] is for mature people whose faculties have been trained by practice to distinguish good from evil." There it is. The practice of godliness leads to the life of godliness. It makes godliness "natural." If you *practice* what God tells you to do, gradually the obedient life will become a part of you. There is no simple, quick, easy or instant way to godliness.

3. Yesterday you made a list of desires to deny. You began working on these. Today take that same list (if you didn't write it out, then do so right away—we'll be using it tomorrow and Friday too!) and plan specifically how to deny (say no to) another one of these desires today. Lay out your plan in the (now familiar) if . . . then fashion:

If _____

_____ [occurs],

then I plan to _____

_____

_____

Evening Checkup

1. Now, you have worked on daily denial of two sinful desires. Talk to God about your progress.
2. Ask for help to overcome the rest.

Week Two   Thursday

Morning

Today and tomorrow will be different.
1. Each day take up a new desire to deny and work on it.
2. Continue to work on the previous ones too.
3. For each desire work out an if . . . then plan of attack.

Now, read the following:

Practice

Practice itself is indifferent; it can work either as a blessing or as a curse, depending upon *what* you have practiced. It is what you feed into your life that matters—just like the data fed into a computer. A computer is no better than the data with which it operates. The end product is good or bad according to the raw material provided for it. That is just like habit. In II Peter 2:14, Peter speaks about people whose hearts are *"trained* in greed." Trained is the same word that Paul used in I Timothy 4:7 (*gymnazo*), the word from which *gymnastics* comes. A heart that has been *exercised* in greed is one that has faithfully practiced greed so that greediness has become natural. Without consciously thinking about it, such a person "automatically" behaves greedily in various situations where the temptation is present.

Since God has made you this way—with the capacity for living according to habit—you must consciously take a hard look at your life. You must make conscious—and carefully examine your unconscious—responses. You must become aware of your life patterns and evaluate them by the Word of God. What you learned to do as a child you may be continuing to do as an adult. Pattern by pattern you must analyze and determine whether it has developed from practice in doing God's will or whether it has developed as a sinful response. There is only one way to become a godly person, to orient your life toward godliness, and that means pattern by pattern. All the old sinful ways, as they are discovered, must be replaced by new patterns from God's Word. That is the meaning of disciplined living. Discipline first requires self-examination, then it means crucifixion of the old sinful ways (saying no daily), and lastly, it involves practice in following Jesus Christ's new ways by the guidance and strength that the Holy Spirit provides through His Word. The biblical way to godliness is not easy or simple, but it is the solid way.

Evening Checkup

1. Be thorough in searching out patterns and desires. Carefully analyze these biblically. You do not want to deny desires that are true and right. If you have any difficulty in this analysis, seek help.
2. Think about your progress. Is anything impeding it? If so, what?

_____

What needs to be done about it? _____

_____

_____

_____

3. Ask God to make this a week of significant growth. If you do as this guide suggests, it can be *just that*. Don't miss the opportunity by allowing your desires to keep you from godly discipline!

Week Two   Friday

1. Today, reread and follow points 1-3 in yesterday's assignments.

2. Then study Galatians 5:22, 23 and measure your life against this standard. Don't be discouraged; it is the Spirit's task to produce His fruit. How? What is your part? Write out your answers.

_____

_____

_____

3. Then read this:

Persevere by Grace

When you discipline yourself for righteousness, you don't have to do it alone. It is God who works in you (Philippians 2:13). All holiness, all righteousness, all godliness are the Spirit's "fruit" (Galatians 5:22, 23). It takes nothing less than the power of the Spirit to replace sinful habits with righteous ones, for a ten-year-old or a fifty-eight-year-old. God never said that once a person reaches forty or fifty (or even eighty) he is incapable of change. Remember what Abraham did as an old man (if you don't know, look it up in a concordance). Think about the tremendous changes that God demanded of him in old age. The Holy Spirit can change any Christian, and does.

As a Christian you should never fear change. You must believe in change so long as it is change oriented toward godliness. The Christian life is a life of continual change. In the Scriptures it is called a "walk," not a rest. We can never say (in this life), "I have finally made it." We cannot say, "There is nothing more to learn from God's Word, nothing more to put into practice tomorrow, no more skills to develop, no more sins to be dealt with." When Christ said, "Take up your cross daily and follow me," He put an end to all such thinking. He represented the Christian life as a daily struggle for change. *You* can change if the Spirit of God dwells within you. Of course, if He doesn't, there is no such hope.

Too many Christians *give up*. They want the change too soon. What they really want is change without the daily struggle. Sometimes they give up when they are on the very threshold of success. They stop before receiving. It usually takes at least three weeks of proper daily effort for one to feel comfortable in performing a new practice. And it takes about three more weeks to make the practice part of oneself. But many Christians don't continue even for three days. If they don't get instant success, they become discouraged. They want what they want now, and if they don't get it now, they quit.

Many Christians lack what the Bible calls "endurance"; they give up. Perhaps this very failure is the key to their lack of godliness. You wouldn't have learned to ice skate, you wouldn't have learned to button your shirt or drive an automobile if you hadn't persisted long enough to do so. You learned because you endured in spite of failures, through the embarrassments, until the desired behavior became a part of you. You trained yourself by practice to do what you wanted to learn to do. God says that the same is true about godliness.

35

All of the stress that the Bible puts upon human effort must not be misunderstood; it is talking about grace-motivated effort, not the work of the flesh. Effort apart from the Holy Spirit doesn't produce godliness. Rather, it is through the power of the Holy Spirit alone that you can so endure. Of your own effort, you may persist in learning to skate, but you will not persist in the pursuit of godliness. A Christian does *good works* because the Spirit first works in him.

Now the work of the Spirit is not mystical. The Holy Spirit's activity often has been viewed in a confused and confusing manner. There is no reason for such confusion. The Holy Spirit Himself has plainly told us how He works. He says *in* the Scriptures that He ordinarily works *through* the Scriptures. The Bible is the Holy Spirit's Book. He inspired it. He moved its authors to write every wonderful word that you read there. This is His book; the sharp tool by which He accomplishes His work. He did not give us the Book only to say that we could lay it aside and forget it in the process of becoming godly. Godliness does not come by osmosis. Your own ideas and efforts will never produce it. There is no easier path to godliness than the prayerful study and obedient practice of the Word of God. That's why you have been following this devotional workbook.

It is by willing, prayerful and persistent obedience to the requirements of the Scriptures that godly patterns are developed and come to be a part of us. When we read about them, we must then ask God by His grace to help us live accordingly. The word *grace* has several meanings in the Bible, one of which is "help." When we ask, "Lord, help us to follow Christ daily in His Word and to become like Him," the Holy Spirit "helps" us to do so. The Holy Spirit gives help when His people read His Word and then step out by faith to do as He says. He does not promise to strengthen us unless we do so; the power often comes *in the doing.*

Evening Checkup

1. Pray about today, especially in light of the above. Commit yourself to the practice of disciplined godly living in the Spirit.
2. Even though you will leave this week's study for a new one next week, don't stop doing what you have begun. That is the essence of disciplined living: consistent, prayerful regularity.

Week Two   Saturday
(Any convenient time)
EVALUATION!

1. This could have been
   A. One of the most exciting weeks of change or
   B. One of the most frustrating weeks in your life—

   (Which was it? _____). It depends
   on how you have followed directions (of course, it might have
   been neither if you didn't pay much attention).
2. What has happened to you through your encounter with God in
   His Bible this week? (be excruciatingly honest):

   _____

   _____

   _____

   _____

3. What led to this? _____

   _____

   _____

4. What could have happened differently? _____

   _____

   _____

   _____

5. What went right, and why? _____

_____

_____

6. What went wrong, and why? _____

_____

_____

7. What have you determined to do about it? (If nothing, then think, pray and study the Scriptures to come to such decisions.)

_____

_____

_____

8. Talk to God about what you have learned from all this.
9. Plan for tomorrow. Ask God to bless your pastor as he ministers God's Word. Pray for those who will receive the message, and pray also (but less) for yourself. Read Matthew 13:18-23 in preparation for the message, noting that the point of the parable has to do with *how one hear's God's message. Prepare to hear and heed.*

Week Three   Sunday

1. Sunday! Time for a fresh start. There is no better way than to get dressed, pray and go to church (take this book along).

2. Church School—relax; keep this book closed; take no notes.

3. *Morning Service:*

   A. Jot down any truths or applications that appear in the Scripture reading and in the sermon:

      1 _____

      2 _____

      3 _____

      4 _____

      5 _____

   B. What was the purpose of the sermon (i.e., how did the preacher intend to change you)? _____

      _____

      _____

4. Afternoon (at home): what truths from the above list would be guiding principles to apply to your life throughout the coming week? (list by number) _____.

   How? _____

   _____

Evening Service:

5. Do the same as you did this morning under 3A and 3B:
   A. Truths and applications:

   1 _____

   2 _____

   3 _____

   4 _____

   5 _____

   B. Purpose of the sermon: _____

   _____

   _____

6. Spend time tonight before going to sleep, asking God's blessing on the week to come. Look forward, not backward: remember, this is the first day of the next week of your life!

Week Three   Monday

Morning

1. By now, if you have faithfully pursued all of the studies and made the personal applications suggested, you will have (a) experienced some significant changes and (b) you will be starting to feel at home with your regular devotions. That's good; but you're not finished yet! This is only a beginning, and you cannot coast on yesterday's momentum. So if you've begun to move the huge snowball, don't quit just when you are beginning to succeed; instead push all the harder. NOW IS YOUR OPPORTUNITY.

2. So far, these studies have been centered on *you* in relationship to God. It would be a mistake to think that you could go on with such a focus for long. I don't want to establish any such pattern in your devotions. So this week we are going to focus on how you can be a blessing to others. Read Philippians 2:3-13.

3. What are the two main truths in verses 3 and 4? _____

_____

_____

4. How did Christ exhibit these in His life and death (vss. 5-13)?

_____

_____

5. How may you do so today? For whom? _____

_____

41

6. Read this:

Shining Lives

Christians, just like their non-Christian neighbors, suffer from unresolved personal problems. They are turning in droves to counselors of all sorts. Pastors are overburdened by husbands or wives threatening to dissolve marriages, by parent/teen struggles, and by interpersonal conflicts among various members of their flocks. There is immense power abroad in the church today, but much of it is being drained off by these energy-wasting difficulties. If even a small proportion of the energy of God's people that is now consumed in anxiety, worry, guilt, tension, anger and resentment were able to be released into productive activity for the kingdom of God, the world soon would know that Jesus Christ is at work today. Sadly, instead, the world still searches for the answer to its problems, seeing little or no difference in the lives of professed Christians.

Yet, potential for untold change now exists; God has amassed an enormous amount of virtually untapped resources. Were the holes in the barrel, through which power is being lost, repaired, the effect would be overwhelming. One necessary preliminary to any real impact upon those around you who do not know Christ is to become the sort of Christian whose life shines. (Read Matthew 5:16.) But shining lives today are rare. The lives of Christians are shot through with the same attitudes found outside the church. Christians look too much like the world. God has told us that usually it is not our teaching or belief that first makes an impression on others; rather, as Peter explained to Christian wives, they would have to win their unsaved husbands without talk by *demonstrating* their faith in daily living (I Peter 3:1, 2ff.). What Peter told wives holds true elsewhere: when others *see* Christianity shining in biblical behavior, they will be ready to hear about it in biblical words. Let your light shine!

7. Ask God to show you some way(s) to shine before others today. (Look for opportunities to put truths *you already know* into practice today.) It may be a blue Monday for many. Don't hide your candle (Christ, the Light in you) under a bushel.

Evening Checkup

1. What opportunities for shining did you have today? List:

_____

_____

_____

_____

_____

2. How did you do in them? _____

_____

_____

_____

3. Did something obscure your light? What? What must be done to remove the obstacle?

_____

_____

_____

_____

4. Pray about this matter in the most appropriate way. Thank God for the opportunities He gave you.

Week Three   Tuesday

Morning

1. The sun may or may not be shining today, but you should! Regardless of the weather, let your light shine.
2. Shining lives (those that exhibit the fruit of the Spirit described in Galatians 5) lead to opportunities to help other Christians whose light is sputtering. Read Galatians 6:1, 2.
3. Now read this:

You Can Help Others Change

Christians everywhere must begin to straighten out their lives and their homes before God and one another. Then in the spirit of gentleness (humility, rather than superiority) they also may begin to minister to one another. That is the background for helping others to change. Now explore this statement: God has obligated Christians to minister to one another as counselors. (Read Galatians 6:1.)

Counseling is not unknown in the Bible. Galatians 6:1, 2 is explicit: each individual, as God gives him occasion, is to *restore* his brother. He may not remain disengaged. Whenever, in the providence of God, he discovers (not looks for) a brother caught in any sin from which he seems unable to extricate himself, he is obligated to help. Staying alert for problems and looking for problems are two distinct stances.

A large number of passages in the New Testament show that this practice was universally taught by the apostles. Many of these passages contain the key words "one another," and many of the "one another" verses refer to exhortation, encouragement, restoration, admonition, rebuke and the giving of other sorts of counsel. What is of greatest importance is that most of them are concerned not with pastors, who are required to counsel as a life calling, but with individual, everyday, man-in-the-pew Christians.[1] Can you help somebody today?

---

1. As an additional optional study, using a concordance, look up all the passages that speak of what Christians must do for "one another."

4. How are you to help a brother or sister who is in trouble?

    _____

    _____

5. Notice especially, you are to *restore*. What do you think that means?

    _____

    How could you best go about this? _____

    _____

    _____

6. Don't miss the condition "in meekness." To go in any other way would harm rather than help. To go that way can *never* harm, even if the other refuses and rejects help. (Look up "meekness" in a Bible dictionary.)

7. Finally, notice the warning. What is it? _____

    _____

    How would that apply to you? _____

    _____

    _____

8. Pray that God will make you meek (a concerned gentleness with no sense of superiority) and that you will recognize opportunities to restore a brother.

Evening Checkup

1. God may not have sent any occasions for restoring another today. What could be one good reason?

45

_____

_____

_____

Can you think of another? _____

_____

What must you do about it? _____

_____

_____

2. Pray hopefully and especially ask for meekness and strength (meekness is not weakness).

Week Three   Wednesday

Morning

1. A lovely day? Well, whether it is or not, it can be a lo*ving* day. And, if it is, it will turn out to be love*ly* also!
2. Read Matthew 22:30-40. In one sentence tell what Jesus says to do for your neighbor.

_____

_____

3. Now check your answer against this:

Does the Bible Teach Self-Love?

When Christ commanded you to love your neighbor (Matthew 22:34-40), He intended to say exactly that and nothing else. Yet psychologizing Christians have tried to add a third and even more basic commandment: love yourself. Some go so far as to claim that unless a person first learns to love himself properly, he will never learn to love his neighbor. Don't believe it!

The argument sounds somewhat plausible at first: How can one love another unless he knows how to love himself? Yet if he thinks (wrongly) that a practice is desirable for himself, he may urge it upon his neighbor *to his injury.*

A moment's reflection shows the fallacy. The Scriptures, not one's personal experience, must tell you how to love another. You cannot go wrong in loving another when you do what the Bible says.

When Christ said love your neighbor as yourself, He did not mean to do for him what you do for yourself. Instead (as in Christ's "first" commandment) the stress in the "second" is upon the *intensity* of the love rather than upon the identity of the action: the second is *like* the first. The words, "as yourself," in the second parallel the phrase, "with all your heart," in the first. The emphasis is not upon the content of the love (that is found in the commandments them-

47

selves), but upon its fervency: "Love as *enthusiastically* as you love yourself." Beyond this, the fact that Christ distinguishes only "two commandments" (vs. 40) itself is decisive.

Psychologizing the passage leads to pernicious errors: (1) God's Word is misrepresented; (2) one's own life rather than God's Word becomes the standard for behavior; (3) endless speculation over matters like proper and improper "self-love" and "self-concept" is generated. It is very dangerous to make a big point over that about which Christ made no point at all (indeed, He explicitly excluded it by the words "two" and "second").

People who try to love themselves will find instead that they are spinning their wheels. Much time and energy can be wasted trying to strengthen egos. Not one word in the Scriptures encourages such activities. They are as futile as the pursuit of happiness. A good self-concept never arises from seeking it directly. Like happiness, it is the by-product of loving God and one's neighbor. The Christian who concentrates on those two commandments will have little problem with the "third," because Jesus said, "Whoever finds his life will lose it, and whoever loses his life for my sake will find it" (Matthew 10:39).

4. Who are some of your neighbors? (Read Luke 10:29-37 to determine who a neighbor is.) List some you will see today:

A _____

B _____

C _____

D _____

E _____

5. How (specifically) could you show love to each of them? (Remember, love begins with giving.

A _____

B _____

C _____

D _____

E _____

6. Pray about those you will see today. Ask God to give you opportunity to show love toward them. What do you have to give to them (time? the gospel? concern? possessions? other

_____)

Evening Checkup

1. How did you do? _____

_____

_____

2. What was the response from your neighbor? _____

_____

_____

3. Did you show love that was as fervent, as intense, as the love you

   show for yourself? _____

_____

_____

4. Ask God to help you to continue to show love; and to do it with fervor.

49

Week Three   Thursday

Morning

1. Well, you've been thinking about how to do good to others. Yesterday you attempted to show love to your neighbors.

2. Did you know how to show love? _____

   _____

   _____

3. Biblical love is not a *feeling* first; rather it is *giving* first. Read John 3:16; Galatians 2:20; Ephesians 5:25, 28, 33; Luke 6:27, 32, 33, 35; Romans 12:20. In all these passages, love involves *giving*.

4. List below persons to whom you can give something that you have that they need:

Person	*What to Give*

_____

_____

_____

5. You can give whether you feel like it or not. The more you in-
vest your time, your concern, your interest, your energy in
another, the sooner your feelings will fall in line (where your
treasure is your heart will be also; *heart* means the whole inner
person, including feelings). Don't wait to give until you feel like
it. Give because you want to please God by obeying Him.
6. Pray about this and go do it. Love begins by doing.

Evening Checkup

1. What did you give to whom? How did your neighbor respond to

the love you showed him/her? _____

_____

_____

2. If the response was poor, that doesn't matter; don't be discouraged. What you did wasn't done for a response; it was done to
please God. That is what counts.
3. This has been quite a day if you have really begun to *give* of
yourself. Thank God for it; confess any failures, other sins, etc.,
and ask for strength to go on loving others by doing good toward
them.

Week Three   Friday

Morning

1. Loving others is an exciting activity when done biblically. Let's do some more things today that will help you learn to love.
2. Perhaps by now you have discovered that loving—like all other things that are done well—takes time and thought. You have to consider *what* to do and *how* to do it.
   That is what Hebrews 10:24 is all about.
3. Read this verse and think about it. Notice: one loving thing to do is to stimulate *others* to love and good works. You are to give thought to ways of doing so. In the space below, record as many possible ways as you can think of to stimulate others to love and good (literally, "fine") deeds:

4. Now choose one or two suggestions from your list and, today, prayerfully put them into practice. If you do not meet a Christian brother or sister in the ordinary course of the day's activity, you may have to write, phone or pay a visit to someone.

Evening Checkup

1. Well, love costs, doesn't it? You found that out today. God's love cost His Son; Christ's love cost His life. They gave to you. Your love today cost you some thought, time, and energy. But it was worth it if you really were able to stimulate and encourage another Christian, wasn't it?
2. Thank God for love. Tell Him you love Him. Decide how you can give yourself to Him: Read Romans 5:5. Ask Him to continue to pour out His love into your heart.

Week Three   Saturday

Evaluation Time!

1. You have discovered that love is more than emotion—or did you?

    _____

    _____

    _____

2. Do you still have questions about love or about how to love?
    Write these out and over the days to come search out the biblical
    answers (ask your counselor or someone else for help if needed):

    Questions   *Biblical Answers*

3. God expects you to love others and to love Him. Do you? If so, tell Him so. If there are problems standing in the way of your love toward God,

A. Tell Him about them.

B. Ask His help in solving them.

C. Search the Scriptures (with help from another Christian, if necessary) for the biblical answers to them.

4. How did love change your life this week? _____

_____

_____

GO ON LOVING OTHERS EVERY DAY OF EVERY WEEK FROM NOW ON!

Week Four   Sunday

1. Sunday! Time for a fresh start. There is no better way than to get dressed, pray and go to church (take this book along).

2. Church School—relax; keep this book closed; take no notes.

3. *Morning Service:*

   A. Jot down any truths or applications that appear in the Scripture reading and in the sermon:

      1 _____

      2 _____

      3 _____

      4 _____

      5 _____

   B. What was the *purpose* of the sermon (i.e., how did the preacher intend to change you)? _____

      _____

      _____

4. Afternoon (at home): What truths from the above list would be guiding principles to apply to your life throughout the coming week? (list by number) _____.

   How? _____

5. *Evening Service:*

   Do the same as you did this morning under 3A and 3B:
   A. Truths and applications:

   1 _____

   2 _____

   3 _____

   4 _____

   5 _____

   B. Purpose of the sermon: _____

   _____

   _____

6. Spend time tonight before going to sleep, asking God's blessing on the week to come. Look forward, not backward: this is the first day of the next week of your life!

Week Four   Monday

Morning

1. This is your last week in this book. You have been involved in an intensive, life-changing experience if you have carefully followed the studies and done the assignments from the past three weeks.
2. Now it is time to wean you from this study guide, to help you to learn how to study the Bible yourself and to give yourself daily assignments growing out of what you have read.
3. Read II Timothy 3:15-17 again. The Scriptures have two purposes: (1) To show people how to be saved; (2) To show them how to change in ways that please God. Now that you are saved, you should use the Bible for the second purpose in all your devotions. (You will use it for the first purpose in evangelism.)
4. O.K., using II Timothy 3:15-17, in the space below write out your own assignments from the passage (at least one to follow today, together with a "how to" assignment, and a prayer assignment appropriate to it. (Turn back to Week One's assignment for a model.)

Evening Checkup

1. How did you do? _____

   _____

2. If you had problems, go back over the previous lessons again and see how it is done. Model your assignments after those.
3. Pray that God will help you to learn how to do these things on your own.

Week Four   Tuesday

Morning

Here is your passage for today: James 4:13-17. Study it and run with it on your own. In the space below write yourself directions and assignments modeled on what you have been doing the past three weeks. Then follow them as you did yesterday.

Evening Checkup

1. Tougher? Yes, but it is important for you to learn how to work on your own.
2. Tonight, I shall even allow you to write out your checkup questions for yourself. Do so in the space below. So, you see, we are almost saying goodbye.

Week Four   Wednesday

Morning

You're entirely on your own from here on (of course, you never *really* are— read Philippians 4:13; I John 2:26, 27). Select your own study passage, write directions, assignments, etc. There are other helps that you should know about. Turn to the back cover and you will find a bibliography for a layman's mini Bible study library. Get these books and learn to use them.

Evening Checkup

Week Four   Thursday

Morning

1. All yours again!

Evening Checkup

1. If you're having trouble—get help; don't give up. Do the best you can. Don't leave any page blank. Turn back to previous assignments for your model.

Week Four   Friday

Morning

1. Last day. Make it a good one!

Evening Checkup

Week Four   Saturday

Evaluation!

1. Do your own (turn back for a model).

Well, you're through! No, you've just begun. Why stop here? Continue to select passages and discover how they can change your life. Take paper and make yourself your own weekly workbooks. Save all of them. Over the years you will deposit valuable material in these to which you will want to refer again and again.

God bless you!

In the following space your counselor may wish to write up a brief evaluation of your work thus far.

_____   _____
Date   Counselor's Signature

The Laymen's Mini Guide to Bible Study Helps

Bibles

> The New American Standard Bible
> The Berkeley Version of the Bible
> The New Testament in Everyday English
>   (or The Christian Counselor's New Testament)

Concordance

> Strong's Exhaustive Concordance

Bible Dictionaries

> The New Bible Dictionary
> Halley's Pocket Bible Dictionary

Commentaries

> The New Bible Commentary
> Individual volumes on each book (ask your pastor for good
>   titles)